Surmai Shaamein

(An Anthology of Poems and Stories)

Deepti 'Dariyadili'

DIAMOND BOOKS

www.diamondbooks.in

Publisher : **Diamond Pocket Books (P) Ltd.**
X-30, Okhla Industrial Area,
Phase-II, New Delhi-110020
Phone : 011-40712200
E-mail : wecare@diamondbooks.in
Website : www.diamondbooks.in
Edition : 2025

Surmai Shaamein *(An Anthology of Poems and Stories)*
Author - *Deepti 'Dariyadili'*

Surmai Shaamein

Deepti 'Dariyadili'

All day in a garden,
We would lie under a flowering tree,
Quietly telling each other things,
Listening to each other.
Flowers would keep falling from the tree
Falling continuously
The flowers would touch
our hands sometimes
Sometimes kissing the lips
And their fragrance mixing with our breath,
Even mixing with our thoughts.
The circumstances were ignorant,
Yet fate perhaps did know
That some day
These three days of our life,
Three ages they may become.
IMROZ

Mine and your hair

Blowing in the air,

Telling stories

Creating history

Fluttering pages

A gale would come

And would flow away

The collective; Mine

And your reflections

In all four directions

Far and far!

Very far away!!!

IN LOVE FOR LIFE,
LOVE'S PHILOSOPHY,
OLD WORKS
IN A NEW LIGHT!

'Surmai Shaamein' is an incredible book that takes you from the real world to the imaginary world.

Narender Kumar Verma
Publisher
Diamond books

Deepti Verma: A Brief Intro

Deepti Verma, a literary prodigy, was born on May 27, 1973, in Jhansi, Bundelkhand province, in the home of Mrs. Param Devi Verma, wife of Dr. Ram Ratan Verma, and began writing poetry at the age of nine. In no time, the light of her name began to spread everywhere.

She aced all of your tests from high school to post-graduation and wowed everyone with your talent in numerous cultural programs such as Kavi Sammelan, Antyakshari, dance, and plays. She made Jhansi proud by performing exceptionally in 'Independence Quiz 1988' organized at district, divisional, and provincial levels. She received special qualification in post-graduate degree in "Musical Instrumentation." She married Engr Premchandra Verma, an officer with an ardent, diligent, and affectionate nature, on March 13, 1999.

Since she received her Master's degree in Music after studying Hindi, Deepti's writing and poems have had a constant rhythmic pulsation. All India Radio Jhansi broadcasted lectures and poems with the honor of 'Bundelkhand's budding poetess' after being impressed by her poetry and presentation.

I wish that after the release of the first book 'Dil Dariya Hai,' the second work 'Surmai Shaamein,' based on your unique poems and stories will also gain popularity among readers.

अवनी

अवनीन्द्र सिंह, आई. ए. एस.)
आयुक्त, विद्यालय शिक्षा
पाश्चिम बंगाल सरकार
7वाँ तल, विकास भवन, साल्ट ले
सेक्टर-2, कोलकाता

“Deepti’s latest work, ‘Surmai Shaamein’, will go down in poetry and narrative tradition as a watershed moment”

‘Surmai Shaamein’ is Deepti ‘Dariyadili’s second book, and it includes both free verse poetry and some of her own short stories. Here, the manuscript for ‘Surmai Shaamein’ is in front of my eyes, but Deepti, a poetess and writer, is also altering the contour of her face in a variety of ways like a movie playing in front of my eyes. I remember the times when poetry readings and poetry gatherings used to happen while Engr. Premchandra Verma, Deepti’s husband, worked at the Jhansi Polytechnic College. I occasionally took time away from my hectic schedule to attend these gatherings, and it was at such events that I first discovered Deepti Ji’s gift for poetry and writing in all of its varied forms.

Five years after the release of her first poetry book, “Dil Dariya Hai,” Deepti decided to add the surname “Dariyadili” to her name since poetry lovers praised it so highly. Since then, a sizable amount of water has flowed via the Ganga and Betwa. Deepti ji’s poetry attained those heights in a short amount of time in Jhansi, where the Betwa flows. And when Deepti ji’s husband Premchandra Verma was appointed as the principal of the Banaras Polytechnic College, the presence of Maa Ganga and art-culture, literature, and in this city of music catapulted

Dipti's poetry to the dizzying heights. To achieve such acclaim, any other litterateurs have to make a long journey over the years. Premchandra Verma Ji is now enhancing the position of Mahoba Polytechnic College Principal. Mahoba is also the home and workplace of authors and heroes, and the song "Aalha" that was composed here holds a special position in poetry and music tradition.

Deepti Ji's personality contains several facets worthy that could be interpreted separately. For example, while absorbing the entire earth into her personality, she doesn't only attempt to verbalize the dispersed nature and culture at every step but also steps into every opportunity to help the marginalized and the helpless people. I've witnessed her so many times passing over a 500 rupee note in place of a 50 rupee fare to cab drivers or small merchants and then proceeding without taking the remaining amount. People are sometimes perplexed since they frequently demonstrate abstention from receiving freebies. Deepti Ji then convinces them with her gesture, "Keep it, this is not freebie." Similarly, I've observed her lavishing love and attention on helpless animals and birds on several occasions. So many such stories are etched in my memory that I'm afraid to start writing them for fear of deviating from the main theme.

Anyway, Deepti Ji has provided me with the manuscript of her published work so that I may express something by using her work as the platform for my writing. That is why I will extensively discuss with you about her personality in another time. Deepti Ji is an epitome of a creative poetic personality, and the element of poetry or narrative has been interwoven into her beliefs and behavior. As previously said, she possesses several such characteristics that set her apart from the rest. Her prose and poetry writings mirror her personality traits. Now, notice at the very beginning of her collection, she has written-

In Love for Life
Love's Philosophy
Old Works
In a new light

If we dig into the depths of poetry, we will find the entire philosophy of love and life contained in these sentences. Be it a poet or a writer, he either turns incidents into events or produces compositions by turning events into incidents, but in the case of Deepti Ji, when she turns incidents into events and when events become incidents into poetry or stories, readers and listeners frequently do not realize because Deepti Ji performs this job with remarkable skill and intelligence. Her creations are ideologically driven, yet there is no uniformity. This is the consistency that distinguishes incidents from events. Her poetry doesn't follow the conventional style and pattern as she has always revolted against this. One of the reasons for this is that her poetry is ideological, and each poem has elements of self-happiness in some form or another. I feel that it is impossible to write beautiful poems while strictly adhering to the grammatical principles of poetry as well as pingal or meter. Because of the compulsion of the verse in the poem, the quality of lyricism comes in it, but the essence of the poem is left behind owing to the restrictions imposed by language and grammar. Deepti ji always walks deeply holding this essence of the poem so that her pen does not deviate from the ideological and philosophical path of poetry and reality remains alongside originality in poems and stories. Yes, despite abandoning rhyme in poetry writing, she makes a concerted effort to keep metrical and rhymed harmony in her poetic matter and style, which results in no loss of rhythm in the poems, and these poems are in the same form when read and heard. I have read her earlier published collection 'Dil Dariya Hai' since Deepti ji had authorized me to write critical remarks on it, which continues to be published in several famous newspapers and journals, including 'Dainik Jagran'. It has been published from time to time and along with Deepti ji's poems and stories, various stations of Akashvani and Doordarshan have also broadcast them. Deepti Ji wanted me to study the manuscript of her new collection 'Surmai Shaamein' thoroughly before commenting on it. Even if she had said no, I would have done more or less the same. Because till now I have written comments on about a dozen ghazal collections, but it is not in my literary culture to write anything without thoroughly reading it.

'Surmai Shaamein' is a love poem, but other compositions included in the work also depict the storms of life, nature, and love and the miseries in their path, and these miseries turn into pleasant feelings in the end. Deepti ji has done this in both verse and prose form, because there are few litterateurs who, along with verse, have the same mastery in prose writing. Whenever a writer who creates poetry writes prose, then in that prose also the flow of poetry can be seen easily. The same has happened in the poems and stories of "Surmai Shaamein'. This work has been divided into two sections — 'A' and 'B' and both sections contain a beautiful fabric of poetry and story. The poems of Section 'A', 'You, me and the Moment', 'Tinted Weather', 'On the Wings of Evening', 'Seasons and the Song', and the story 'Love Affair' deeply affect the inner mind. There is also the poem 'Surmai Shaamein' in this section, about which it is needless to say that it has been given the form of the title of the work because of being very influential. The titles of the poems show that these have been written in unconventional ways while incorporating originality in them.

Compositions like 'Destinations are not easy' and 'Desire of mind' in section 'B' makes the mind as well as the brain happy.

The outer cover and inner page of the work have a different kind of attraction, which has been made possible by the combination of black and white shapes and images matching them with poems and stories.

Here too, the art sense of the poet-narrator is additionally visible.

As a matter of fact, Literature, art, and music are three different colors of fine arts and if a worshiper of any of these arts interferes with any other fine art as well, then it should be considered as her additional quality. This brings out her original art. Something similar has happened here also; the matching pictures have made those poems of the poetess even more alive, which already seem to be speaking because of the selection of words and language according to the subject. The art expressed on the cover page of the work and its concept is the result of thinking of my friend and country's famous painter Bhai Kishan Soni ji and if I say that due to the presence of Bhai Kishan Soni ji in the work, its beauty, importance and collectability has increased manifold, then it should not be considered as an exaggeration in any form. During the performance of her art, Kishan ji has not only protected the poetic work contained in the work from every point of view but also tried that his art should be close to the thinking of the poet and the storyteller.

In the end, I can say with full confidence that after the release of her first poetry collection 'Dil Dariya Hai', this fast-emerging poetess and story writer Deepti 'Dariyadili' had secured her place in the minds and hearts of connoisseurs of Poetry and Literature, whereas after the publication of

'Surmai Shaamein', the world of poetry and literature will accept him as an established constellation of poetry and literature. In this, I have no doubt whatsoever. I wish, this thought and vision of mine about her emerge meaningful on the ground of reality!

- Rajkumar Anjum

Honorary Features Editor

'Dainik Jagran' Jhansi

Contact: 9415946102

To the readers

My second attempt at poems and stories on the lines of the first collection 'Dil Dariya Hai' is 'Surmai Shaamein', in the composition of which the words of a film song, "*yadon ke sab jugnu jungle mein rehte hain.* (All the fireflies of memories live in the forest)" started floating on the lips while carving 'sea evenings'. Almost everyone must have lived these moments, full of mutual love with their fellow travelers with their desires in their lives.

This is the trust of two people and the 'faith' between them—

It is a relation of two identities, of two people born out of the womb of one feeling. It is born, grows, but does not grow old.

But those people, who have prayed this river and sea, know—

It is neither profit nor loss. There is neither greed nor custom. There is no ritual; there is no worship of the temple. It lives in those two sacred people and dies with them; it cannot live alone; it is not even one-sided. It is the twin birth of a union of two people.

In the end, I would like to say to the readers who have liked my first book 'Dil Dariya Hai' with great enthusiasm; the second and last part of the story 'Love Affair' described in it has been compiled in the composition 'Surmai Shaamein' which is in your hands. The 'poetry born of separation' described in section 'B' has been included keeping in mind the other interests of all of you.

D. Verma

Deepti 'Dariyadili'

Contents

Section 'A'

Section 'B'

Section
'A'

-: Love Devotee :-

Fireflies twinkling,
Smoke trail
Trembling leaves
Deserted road
Got up
Come to
Give your
Concern.
It's all about
Love moments,
In blazing chest,
Oblivious to the times
Got together,
Spread wings
Under blue skies
Spreading a canopy.
Building a house

Golden dream

Lonely home

Birds chirping

Calm core

Love devotee

Under the kadamba tree

Silence! Silence!

-: You, me, and the pause moments :-

Standing next to me

Like the vibration of the soul,

Bearing witness with me

Seeing like a mirror.

Golden pictures

And beautiful

Dunes

And amazing

Twittering

Of a couple,

Together

Holding hands

Cracking

Dune

Hugging

Gliding

Keep on moving;

In steps

Together.

On the sand

Like ringing the anklet

Desert

Becomes sea

Of the sand

Deposits become

Of straws

Whirlwinds rise

All around

And far away!

With me

He

Kept standing

Being like

My shadow

Play like

Movies

Everything goes

Touching around

Further away!! Distant!!

-: A noon; after years :-

Citadel's crooked
rocky road
gathering of
Bats and owls.
The walls of stones
all asleep,
raw land
full of dampness
and bats,
Yet there are
inner feelings
of fragrances,
inside you and me.
Somewhere there is moss
and greenery,
somewhere

bed of flowers

or

places full of grass.

Slumbering rough walls,

years and years

ago

scent of

wind

lingered there

continuous,

never still

always flowing,

It flies

away and far

with the

the breath of

the lovers

pneumatic

in all directions.

Years and
years later,
there's you and me
still standing there;
at noon
under the sunshine
filtered through
leaves like
a satin embroidery
woven with yarn
and
traversing through
the year,
wind hits
us both
blowing our hairs
telling stories
making history
flipping pages

gale comes

and our reflection

floats together,

far away

Very far!!

-: Tinted Weather :-

Spring season,
and this loneliness.
Tinted weather,
and this embrace.

You and I met,
in that season,
blue, yellow flowers,
bloomed in that season.

How the evening has come-
so intoxicated,
the colors of Rainbow
spread and scattered.
Windy weather
And this east wind.
Tinted weather,
and this embrace.

The queen of evening
came as a bride,
adorning the head
with vermillion.

You and I met,
in that season-
Dreamy flowers,
bloomed in that season.

Weather like jujube
        and this mango-groove
tinted weather
        and this embrace.

-: Wreath and Life :-

Sunlight melted on the
lips of the afternoon.
Waves rose from
the ocean of sand.
When will you come?
Waiting for you dear,
Life should not come
out of the dunes,
some deposits should remain!

Sand's Life, Water's Reflection

The white wall whose plaster had come off had some circular, crooked marks. At some distance, a banyan tree was standing erect, and the sound of tinkling bells was emanating from the temple. At about half past five, the sound of evening prayer was resounding, piercing the desolation from the right side. Natasha spread her legs, hugged herself, and looked at the clock; it was thirty-five minutes past nine. Today was the last day of teaching in the college, but the holidays had started almost from today itself. Looked at the book in front of her, and saw some familiar appendix, then she lay and her eyes started searching in it randomly. The photo of Salim and his armband slid to one side. Peach-colored shirt and gray paint and the young lady in a maroon-colored dupatta along with light green salwar kameez — with how much care and confidence Salim's house was decorated, cursing the bonds of caste and religion.....

Then she heaved a sigh and looked at the clock; it was five minutes past twelve. She poured juice from the jug lying on the tripod and drank almost half the glass. Along with her uneasiness, the heat of the day was also spreading. A little scared of this humid afternoon, she went to the backyard and sat under the neem tree. Somewhere in the distance, melodious voices were being played and Salim's face was coming closer to her face. The dry neem leaves were scattering like the pages of a raw bound book of past life. Salim's autumnal eyebrows, full red lips, and curly hair playing on the forehead, Natasha's youth smelled seductively in his tight arms. Days passed by and nights passed, one sky joined with another, and days, months, and years passed. The calendar on the purple wall kept changing. One day the wall became empty and the calendar of life was torn. Not only the hands of the clock but also the hands of time were moving ahead of Salim and Salim used to return home sooner or later; Tired of waiting, Natasha's eyelids fluttered up and down. When asked, she feigned the same preoccupation, but the truth reflected beyond its forged structure could not hide a lot; after Salim left the house, the desolation of centuries would have been spread in the house, after coming, the quiet silence would spread. The door would creak open and Salim would roll on the bed.

Natasha's existence would have remained isolated on a corner of the bed. Salim would turn carelessly, Natasha would look desperately on his back. Breaking the patience, she would start flowing spontaneously. Salim shook her arms and told her that he wanted to break the relationship with her.

'No, you can't do like this,' Natasha said hoarsely.

'I am fed up after marrying you; do you know how to keep your husband happy? How lonely am I in this house? You are busy with yourself.'

Natasha held Salim with her both hands but Salim said, almost releasing his hand, 'Listen, Natasha, if you want to stay here you can stay. Ragini will be with you or if you want I can send you wherever you want. But uff! I am bored of you. How boring is our relationship now.' Natasha screamed, her wings of dreams were shattered. With tired steps, Natasha turned to the sofa and sat down.

When she woke up from the sleeping ruins of the unconscious mind, it was about four o'clock in the evening, a few drops of sweat had rolled down her forehead, the hour of the hot evening was still left, and the sun, covered with a sheet of bright rays, was shining.

She pulled the chair, folded it, and came into the room, her eyes went to the photo frame of Monalisa hanging on the wall, and the sickly sad pale smile that was carved on her beauty seemed much closer to her smile. She drank water from an earthen pot kept on one side of the room and then covered it with an earthen lamp. Books were scattered on the shelf at some distance in the room. Godrej's almirah had the same color as the bookshelf, an ebony-black wood bed with a mottled bedspread and a tufted pillow, on which Natasha rested, often dusting off the dusty layers of memory, reliving her depressions by keeping refreshed from the flow of her salty tears. It was time for Surekha to come; with her, Natasha's mind used to be happy for a few moments. Her friend's life story was also written on the pages of bitterness, but she was in love with life, she used to talk to life in cool words, even though she was left abandoned by the one she was infatuated with. Surekha used to sit with her during these holidays.

Today, Natasha put her black purse on her shoulder and went to school to teach; when she entered the class the girls got up and greeted her. After finishing the lesson, she came to the staff room, opened the register, and started working. She was feeling thirsty, and when she took water from pitcher, it was not cold. A tingle of pain arose in her head, she opened the lid of three or four pitchers, and the hotness of the water turned out to be the same, she poured three or four sips down her throat and got busy with a reluctant mind.

There was the Directorate of Education in front. With weary feet, she started walking there. Pitchers in the outer chamber often contained cold water. When the sandal was dragged, the nail of her heel came out, and as a result, the heel of the sandal was hanging a little differently. When she put her hand on her head, the hair was wrapped like dry vines on her round face. Some were tangled near the forehead. Her temples were burning with the heat. When she reached the verandah of the directorate, Surekha was coming from the front. She had bundles of notebooks in her right hand and was looking very busy. When she saw Natasha in front, she smiled and hurriedly took the load, came down the stairs, and entered the schoolyard. The verandah of the directorate was cold. It was like a cold shower in the desert. Like the aliphatic banks of the desert river. She opened four pitchers near the poppy straw and saw pure water. After drinking cold water from a gleaming, clear brass mug, Natasha's heavy legs bent down beside the chair. To get rid of fatigue, she spread herself out on the chair. The breath became as cold as ice, in the hot, swollen chest, spread all over the body as fresh glaciers. The dusty, warm layers of memories shrank into the cold folds. She couldn't move with the sandal. After getting some rest, a nap came. She laid her head on the desk. A manly voice broke her sleep as if someone had turned towards her. When she raised her head, she saw a young man with a dark, strong body and a broad saddle.

'Why you are so burdened. Something wrong, please tell me.' Holding on to the *pallu* of the sliding sari, a staggering Natasha stood up and said, 'nothing like that,' and tried to step out by dragging her rattling sandal.

‘Here are some nails in the cupboard; maybe you can walk better,’ said the man, who was almost reaching youth. He said this while throwing his eyes toward the slippers. He brought a weigh, nails, and some things from the teak cupboard. Hesitatingly, Natasha took off her slippers. ‘If it can be fixed, I will try to fix it now; don’t worry,’ he said. Natasha nodded with a slight ‘yes’. Neel’s searched items and heeled slippers got fixed. ‘Take it; you are fine; wear it’, the sympathetic voice emerged again. ‘Thank you’! Natasha said, bowed head in gratitude. The man got stuck and wanted to say something, and she got stuck and went ahead. He had been watching her barren life for days, alone and silent. Sometimes he could see her sleeping peacefully. He was also lonely but used to drown himself in Sumedha’s jokes and activities. He used to take a dip in some water in the heated sand. He kept watching her go away, probably praying for his and her well-being. Not because Natasha was Sumedha’s class teacher, but because Neel’s heart was rising from the weariness of his mind. There was a strange cloud of desolation in their lives. Perhaps the layer of sorrow buried in both was the same. Reshma, with whom he could not even complete the journey of a happy life for a few days, had died in a road accident. Sumedha was the only sign in which he saw the reflection of Reshma. Sumedha also wanted to have a mother like other children. He would take care of her daughter, sings her lullabies, and pats her.

Then he would go and lie down in his room; without Reshma's love and caressing, spending the nights looked harrowing. In the morning, after cleaning the scattered household, baking his bread, and putting it in the lunch tiffin of his daughter. He would spend a lot of time in the office.

The sound of the bell was emanating. When Natasha came out of the classroom after taking the fourth period, Surekha was coming from the front. 'Come Surekha, let us go to the quarters for some time where we can make tea and chat together,' Natasha said, wiping the 'tears' from the corners of her eyes. 'Yes, Natasha, I also have something to understand,' Surekha said. Hand in hand, both friends entered, tearing open the cover of dusk, opened the lock, and entered the kitchen. A faint breeze was coming through the window, giving relief from this restless heat. Surekha took a sip of tea and said, 'at Bahona corner, he has opened a new dispensary. He has just arrived here; he says that his medicine and liquor have healing of the hand. I had gone to take medicine for throat pain, he looks like a cheater, and looks at patients more than anything else. For the first time, he crossed the limit and held my hand. When I abused him after releasing my hand, he said, I am not as swaggerer as you think. I am a respectable person. Anytime I can come to your house and ask for your hand.' Surekha was shy after saying, but there was fear inside. Though she had drunk the cup, she was still holding it in her hand.

Unknowingly, she was scratching the bottom of the cup with her nails. Natasha moved the tripod. Taking the cup she was holding in her hand and placing it on the tripod. Sitting on the bed with her legs folded, she said, 'You have been tricked once, be cautious, this time.' Surekha put the pillow on that wide black bed and spread her legs. Now it is better if Umir feels detachment.' Surekha said that and started thinking seriously. Bitterness came from her mouth, and then she became sleepy.

Natasha peered into the window; darkness was spreading. It was a new moon. The humming of crickets were increasing. Night was dancing wearing anklets, and fireflies were floating here and there on her bodice. Far away, attracted by the light of a lampshade, moths were buzzing beneath it. From a state of mind, it looked as if a small fountain of water was running in the light or raindrops were falling. The far end of the window was surrounded by bushes. The neem-acacia forest here used to spread silence as it loomed large like the blanket of night. Natasha closed the screen of the window and put up the chain; she was feeling that Surekha would sleep here today. They were hungry. She rushed to the fridge. Afternoon's juicy vegetable was already there and she started making tehri in the kitchen. Surekha opened her eyes by rubbing her eyelids. She looked here and there, but Natasha was not there. There was some smell of cooking and the sounds of ladle running were coming from the kitchen. In a short time, pulav was ready and both of them ate and slept.

Today, after returning from school and shopping, she wanted to return to the staff quarter, so she turned towards the road to Tower House. The weather had become pleasant due to light showers, and a cool breeze was blowing. There were trees of chiraul, tamarind, and semal along the side of the road. She was repeatedly balancing her pallu which was waving from the wind coming from the front. Chiraul and other leaves were creaking under the sandals. This creak used to engrave the memories of her bygone days, but this shade of the weather and the sound waves of the cooing cuckoo started spreading in her mind a wholehearted relationship with life. The hustle and bustle of the market could be heard after turning from the corner of the front street.

There were many bags. Two hands from the front caught her bags and greeted her respectfully. Soon her eyes fell on Sumedha, the little girl standing next to her, who was saying 'Good evening, Madam' in a sweet but loud voice. Normally, children say something very fast, 'Good evening, good evening. 'Sumedha daughter' and she looked at her companion, who was holding her luggage very carefully. Natasha did not want to give life a chance. She said in a stern tone, 'Give it to me; I will take care of it.' Neel alias Neelkant felt as if Natasha did not like it. He hesitantly said, 'you are Sumedha's teacher, we also have some duty towards you; May your grace also be on our side. Sumedha talks a lot about you; after three days, Sumedha's birthday is on the twenty-seventh; you must come. Please don't disappoint Sumedha.' Having uttered such a statement, the swarthy build man was holding Sumedha's finger with one arm, and with the other hand, he again took Natasha's luggage and started following her. After reaching home, 'Come' came out of her mouth with difficulty. 'We are in a hurry now' they said. Those people had smooth smiles. They gave her the goods and went ahead. Seeing any man used to make her very angry. Salim had darkened her destiny. She had painted the walls of the heart with this black ink and had turned away from the spark of the lights. Once upon a time, she had lit a lamp in her heart but now she had put it off. That face was very innocent which was close to her now but the woman inside was afraid of sunlight. She wanted to destroy the woman inside her who gets tied to the arms of a man. Perhaps, indeed her friend Surekha was also afraid of these deceptions. Surekha will not come today. She opened the lock. She was feeling sad. There were wrinkles on the plaid sheet that was lying on the bed. Holding it by the corners, she fixed it and placing the luggage on the tabouret and some below, she spread on that ebony black bed. Will she go to Sumedha's birthday or not?

I probably shouldn't go, and I shouldn't promote these things. There was a knock on the door even as she could hardly open her eyes.

Knocking at the door continued. Enough time had passed. It was a bit apprehensive to open but guard was walking around with full security of the staff quarters. The door opened. Sumedha had not come with her father but with some other gentleman; she was telling that she had come with her uncle, but that strong fair man stood aside outside. Sumedha came inside and said with great request, 'Teacher Ji, what will you bring on my birthday, bring my favorite thing.' 'What will you have?' Natasha asked lovingly.

'Had my mother been there, she would have loved me a lot and would have brought me the things of my choice. She would have fed me with things of my choice.'

'What do you want for your birthday tomorrow?'

'I want a pink frock with laces, the rest of the people will bring their kind of gift. Okay teacher, let me go and I nodded and Sumedha left with that

strong fair man, saying teacher ji, bye, bye. I kept looking outside... The watchman rang for ten o'clock that broke my sleepiness, I went to the kitchen after putting a chain on the door, and started peeling eggs quickly. The broth was kept in the afternoon, eggs had to be fried and put in the vegetable and flat bread had to be baked.

I got up early in the morning and prepared the matter to be taught in the class. Wearing a green saree, hanging a black purse on her shoulder, I entered the school premises. Teacher Savita said with waggishness, 'You are looking very pretty today.' Lean and thin Kavita also smiled and I came to eat lunch with her during the interval. 'Hey, do you know Ragini? Did you forget that she was the reason that led Salim to evict you from the home? Unlike you, she was not sensitive and hearted; she forsook her husband for the sake of the second one. I remained silent and not shocked even as I was not able to refresh the old wounds. Seeing her inertia, Savita said a little slowly, 'His factory caught fire and got destroyed. Earnings of years were burnt to ashes; the ready-made business came to a standstill. God punished him a lot. He didn't consider his wife as his wife; his other wife broke the fire of infidelity. I had heard that the other woman was also fed up with his habits. He had the habit of courting women. Now the situation is that his wife doesn't consider it appropriate to stay with him at all. She also

changed her color.' Natasha just listened and she went on talking. 'Here his second wife is being appointed as an Urdu teacher.' Then both of them finished their lunch and got up for the fifth period.

Natasha was neither happy nor sad. Life had played with her jokingly. She had become the subject of peeping smiles, chatter and discussion. Natasha didn't want to remember the time passed, almost none of the time as a result: while returning from school, her steps had taken the way towards the big lake. The weather was pleasant; the cold wind was strong, but now she was in a mood to live like her friend Surekha. She wanted to be her own and maybe live a woman's life.

Engrossed in the chain of thoughts, she sat down obliviously under the dense shade of the banyan tree near the lake. She started humming softly to the rhythm of the rhythmic paddles moving in the lake. The sound of paddles was making noise in the waves of water, a newly married couple was sitting in it, and the young man was standing near the sail, wearing glasses with golden frames. With one leg raised on the deck, the French bearded man with a sharp eye-line was caressing the beauty's open hair with his hands. His face was bent toward the point of view of beauty in a romantic style like a hero of Hindi films. Natasha gazed at the motionless scene through the slits of her silent eyes. Her back was towards her. She was wearing a pink colored silk saree. Natasha, Natasha! Scream came from within telling her 'don't look'. Don't look. Natasha closed her eyelids, and their reflection was captured in the closed eyelids. She opened her eyes trembling, and then had to face carefully to see the side figure of the beauty which she had seen. There was a special identity. A beautiful cloud had settled in the corners of his eyes. 'Hey! With whom is Surekha here, has she gone mad, will she not be tricked again.' tears flow down the cheeks after raining from the eyes. No, Surekha, don't do this again. But the duet singing of the man and the beauty in mutual embrace was heard again. Natasha held her palms to both her ears and closed her eyelids like a relaxation....

As she opened her eyes, the air stopped trembling; the unwanted sight was mesmerizing as if a magician was imprisoning her in the realm of magic. Quickly, she started walking towards the quarter. There was irritation, but the mind was pleasant like the weather.

Yesterday was the 27th of July. Baby Sumedha's innocent words and her father's insistence were ringing in her ears. Once again she put her hands on both ears, she wanted to keep her eyes fixed on the wall hanging in front of the room which used to keep the pins of her hair. She didn't want to disintegrate; she wanted to collect thoughts. Taking a vague decision about whether to go or not, leaning on the pillow placed against the wall, she started preparing the matter to be taught in tomorrow's class. She prepared breakfast early in the morning. After sipping tea and getting dressed, she got ready.

Today Sumedha looked happiest in the class; she bowed down and greeted her first. Natasha nodded gleefully, and the classes continued. Today also, on returning, she went to the market before going home. She bought a nice dhani saree for herself which had embroidery of black bell boots, matching silk blouse and large earrings with tight network in the circle shape. She didn't know, why her hand started wandering on lipstick of pink shades; she chose a lovely shade from them. Hey! She had to buy a pink frock for Sumedha's birthday. I don't know why I bought lipstick; I wouldn't even apply it. After turning around the corner in front, she went to the children's clothes shop. She started seeing pink shades of frocks there. After seeing all, she liked a lacy pink frock.

She got ready after keeping the gift pack aside. She dressed in a dhani saree nicely and started seeing her slim body which still looked young. Then after putting on a light shade make-up and brushing her hair, she put on a hairpin, a tightly woven artificial coil, and carefully fill the lips with the color of the lipstick. She came out of the quarter with the gift pack and locked the door of the house. She took a taxi and reached Sumedha's house; it was far away but the address was simple. The senior accountant was standing outside. He greeted her and brought her to the room with affection. The whole room was decorated with balloons and toffees, the birthday-cake was decorated on the table. There were only a few people comprising more close relatives than guests. Everyone welcomed Sumedha's teacher. A happy Sumedha came to get her favorite birthday gift and hugged Natasha, Natasha's heart was also filled with affection, and she started stroking her head. The whole room started echoing the birthday song. Accountant Neelkant Ji was busy in welcoming them; even without wanting to, his eyes would stop at Natasha's beautiful face and body. When Natasha looked at him, he smiled, but Natasha turned around indifferently and started eating the puris kept on the plate after soaking them with vegetables. But God knows, the desire to look at Neelkant woke up. She slowly turned her neck, and Neel was still smiling as if there was a feeling to hug her, bringing the morning of greenery into the barren life of both of them.

'Hey, you haven't eaten cheese curry, are you eating something or have you fallen asleep standing up,' Savita said. His voice brought Natasha down as if watching a movie theater, which could not have happened in her life. 'Hey, I am like that, did you eat? Today, I am delighted to see you wearing the matching green dress,' Natasha said to her. Then

suddenly the light went off, the heat started spreading in the room, she started moving towards the terrace from where gusts of cold air was coming, but she got scared as if she collided with something and that thing wrapped her in itself. 'Don't panic, I am Neel... Neelkant, you will not fall.' In an instant, she found herself in his arms, fearing to fall from the terrace, she collapsed further into his arms. It was almost full, he was caressing her back. She was feeling the warmth of his hand on her big back. She closed her eyes and Neel placed his lips on her forehead. Soon she stood apart and Neel loosened the shackles. Shivers ran through whole body. This was more intoxicating than that, one evening last night, when she trembled seeing her friend Surekha in the image of a couple. Neelkant put a wrapped paper in his hand. She ran away from there and the paper remained in her hand. She adjusted the saree with care and came to the party room after saving the eyes of the people where Sumedha and others were. It was half past nine in the night. The taxi available at the intersection in front would directly reach to his quarters. She wanted to go but Neel's eyes were searching for her. 'Madam, don't go in the dark,' Neel said, 'that's my habit.' 'But don't leave our place like this.' 'Yes, yes, when Neel is going to leave you, what is your objection, it is not right for a woman to go alone in the dark, ' a middle-aged woman said in an elderly manner. Nothing came out of Natasha's mouth and she sat in the back of Neel's scooter. The roads were silent but there was a stir in both hearts. Natasha was trying to pacify that commotion but Neel's heartbeat was getting uncontrollable. 'Speak up Natasha, Natasha ji you will accept me, you will accept me!!' He spoke suddenly. Natasha couldn't respond, the quarters had come near, and she opened the lock and fell on the bed inside. Neel stopped the scooter and stood for some time, then went away without answer. Natasha could not muster up the courage to open the bundle of papers in her hand. She didn't know when she fell asleep. Neelkant's face was roaming before her eyes when she woke up around three o'clock (in the middle of the night). Pale expression, innocent face. The fountain of love was coming towards her. To stop its flood, she closed her eyes. She closed her eyes, flopped on the bed, turned off the light, and tried to fall asleep.

That night Neel's mind could not remain at peace. He wanted to grow the basil of his heart in the courtyard of his desolate house. What was on Natasha's face? She had big eyes that were like the eyes of his late wife. He had a very restless night tonight. He had spent only two years of married life happily before his wife died in a road accident. In these past seven years, he had not even thought about any woman for marriage. He used to spend his time with baby Sumedha or in loneliness, turned pages of his lonely book which was written with silent words. Yesterday, those silent words came out suddenly. This silent glacier was melting from some days, but today Natasha wants this glacier to build a dam between the two but there was a barrier of 'no'. When she opened eyes in the morning, the bundle of paper given by Neil was still pressed in her fist. The curtain was removed from the window panes and sunlight entered the room. Natasha was awakened somewhat in her sleep by a knock at the door. Saying 'come in', she sat down to sleep and then got up. At this time, the peon used to come to collect the keys to the school bus but she found Surekha standing there. 'Hey Surekha, when did you come? You haven't been here for many days.'

Hiding her happiness, Surekha said, 'I am fine,' then smilingly said, 'Something of yours… I had been very busy. Of late, I had gone to Allahabad. That's all,' she said almost hiding the happiness in her heart.

'I know what your demeanors are.'

'What do you know about me?'

'I saw day before yesterday, only once, looking at that.......' I guessed.

"Yes, Natasha, what you saw was not wrong, the one whom I used to call a swaggerer, doctor, doctor is a good person (suppressing the euphoria of the mind); he is really a very good person. He is doing the engagement ceremony the day after tomorrow; it will be at my house in Allahabad. You have to go with me,' she said, and then took Natasha's hand in her. Then after stopping for a while, she said, 'There is something in yours too, tell me, you too become like me.'

'No, I'm not.'

'So, will you keep mourning all your life?'

Natasha said, 'So, should I romance in the waters like you?' Surekha said chirping, 'With that dude. We are doing that. Let me get married to that shy-one once.'

'No, no Surekha. In this case, we are different.'

"What are you saying, Natasha? You and I are women; we are made of the same soil, a woman's life like a mountain does not pass alone. A woman's salvation is in bondage only."

'I understand your mind a lot, but you are stubborn.'

Natasha began to rub her hands; the bundle clenched in her fists was wet with the sweat of her palms.

"But what is this, Natasha; it must be his secret."

'How can you say that?'

Savita told and some 'idea'... Surekha grabbed the paper and opened it. Something was written in it,

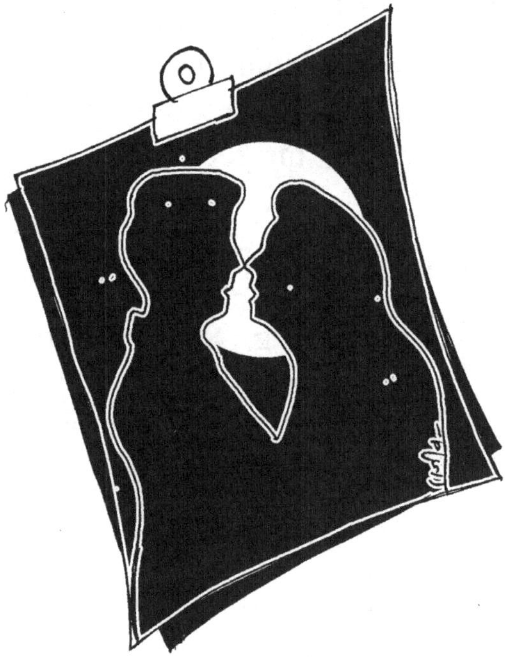

after reading which Surekha's face lit up. She thought that Natasha had also found someone who loved her wholeheartedly, but Natasha cried out of fear. Surekha raised Natasha's chin and said with great caress, "Crazy, you need not cry, good days have come, and luck is knocking at your door. I am going to talk to him about your 'engagement'. Next day, Surekha brought in 'yes' and both friends hugged each other.

A spring of water loomed in the barren depressions.

-: Steady flow :-

The mind
danced like a
peacock in
distant
directions,
His fragrance
mixed
in the air
of that person,
My body
and mind
danced,
My existence
was shaken
like boisterous waves;
Every
moment
gets

scattered on
dreamy wings;
The trail
of promises
and oaths
used to
pass through
the mind,

all around,
The path of
yours and mine,
kept sliding
through the
twisting turns.
Don't know
the direction of
these roads;
But there is a
destination of
infinite love.

-: Your destination :-

I wish I will be yours.
And steal away your songs.
Moments of sweet-smelling
songs here-
the blooming intoxicated
lotus here-
with the wings of desires,
I felt, I can fly away. And steal away...
I wish I will be yours.
And steal away your songs.
The moments of melting,
smoldering breaths here.
Wherever I see you
The clarinets play there.
With the wings in the sky,
I felt I can fly away. And steal away...
I wish I will be yours.
And steal away your songs.

-: Dusk's wings :-

Come and let us make a song
Steal songs from vocal waves.
Steal the white moonlight away
from the rays of the moon.
Decorate the seed-plots
with the flowers of lilies.
Come and let us make a song
Steal songs from vocal waves.
On the smile line of the lips.
Decorate it with melody.
Decorate the courtyard of
our house with blue flowers.
Come and let us make a song
Steal songs from vocal waves.
Under the misty evenings,
Let us settle a world.
On the wings of dusk,
Let us take a flight.
Come and let us make a song
Steal songs from vocal waves.

-: An evening abode :-

The refuge of the evening
deserted and desolated
till far away,
the flower of jasmine,
the dust of gold,
the silver river,
the chains of moonlight,
the strings of pearls
till the body of waves.
On the morning of the beach,
the whistles
of the parrot,
the hanging
mango blossoms,
at this age,
let us be
immature together
and walk hand in hand
so that these
sweet memories of life
are not forgotten!

-: Sky-Sea :-

In the smoke of the clouds,
peeping through
the windows of
sunlight and shade,
how far will
this journey
of the sun go,
playing hide and seek!
The sky's butterflies
on the bush of wind
are nature's peeps,
the instruments of colors,
is decorated on
wings.
The sun is sitting on
the foundation of light,

the sky talks
to the sea,
the corners of
the earth is
decorated with the
sails of the rays,
the carpets of
the waves are spread on
the transparent floor
of the green water,
the forming and deforming
of acacia trees
shine like
the fireflies in
the day
Dear, I and you sitting
in the world
boat
see countless scenes;

The greenery of

the earth and

the light of

the morning

are shining in

the sky of the mind.

-: In the oven of day :-

Melodies stringed
wearing a morning gown
the morning opened the eyelids
embracing string of rays
on Amber's sitar.
Became picturesque, became mellifluent,
Our dreams light up
from the sun's flame, this
in the oven of day.

-: Earth's Son and Sky's Fairy :-

The sky is far away
And the moon is
At a distance.
Like a drop of Moonlight,
It shone like a
Half-star in the light.
Darkness melts
Like a wax
In the mirror of light.
Milky moonlight
Keeps shining
Keeps slipping
On the edge of darkness.
Bright-bright
silver body
Hair fluttering in
the black sky.
Crackling stars in the dress

Galloon of rays
edge-to-edge.
Clouds floating
Like white cotton.
Moonlight white
Moon fairy
Spreading wings.
A mad wanderer
Stretches his arms
Calling her
In the fields, in the barns,
In the streets, in the corridors
On the rocky paths.
How silver fairy
Will come in
Dusty roads,
Walks on clouds
And the moon
Is her house
The Light
Is her lover.

-: Travel's Story :-

Shimmering water
Journey of lake
The paths decided
the course of
these stories.
Bright blossoms
and green water
Grandma used to tell
this story;
How it rained.
From the sky,
the rays of rainbow
of the melting sun.
Monsoon rains
in the blazing sun,
The hem tangled
with the
acacia thorns.

Every moment
it gets scattered
on rainbow wings,
on free winds,
on tangled vines,
On the bowed
delicate vines,
The fickle air
rises slowly,
restless all around.

The land covered
with thorny
bush and flowers,
A bunch of burrus,
the red sage flower,
tell the story of the
journey from
the beginning to
in their own words.

-: Tender but courageous :-

A blue flower
has grown
in the crevices
of the rocks
velvety
with many petals.
It is fully bloomed
on its own.
Loaded with
Dew, beauteous.
Nature's wizard
has filled it with
magic colors;
How after breaking the soil
and coming out of abysm
it has soaked
earth's envelope
with its blue color.

The blue ocean
of the sky
of meditation, trance, inner
consciousness has
colored the
envelope of the earth,
and in this
small space
another sky has
been created.

-: Season and Song :-

The leaves covered
the glistening lake water,
This story of weather
floated in the winds,
Dispersed in the clouds
like a song,
Clouds rained
in the river, in waves,
became your pearl,
In the clamshell of your memories.

Surmai Shaamein {Pleasant Eventides!!!}

I spent a cold evening
with you
on the deserted shore,
My hair like
fringe strands
were getting decorated
in your tangled hair.
Sometimes it used
to scatter on your arms,
on your chest.
Like the moonlight
slipping and hiding
in your loving hands
my glossy face,
Water's edge
delicate waves
Pleasant Eventides!

Merry Christmas

Gray scenery,
On the sky and sea
Advancing darkness
Surmai Shaamein,
Nights of the winter
The open coast,
Me and you
together
On these cold nights,
The clouds of fog
Started weaving
Woolen shawls.
The waves of the sea
Are wrapped
In a gray sheet
Ash-grey evenings!
Wading in the clear water,
The sky getting darker
A shadow image of light.
Beautiful evenings!!
Yellow sunlight
Coming down

From the hood –
Calling out to his beloved.
Getting lost
in the shadows
under the pine trees
hiding in the
green walls of the
lethargic afternoon
sinking in the
quagmire of the day
the advancing darkness.
The dusk keeps
on sliding
the pale-blue evening
keep sinking.
Shattered pearl-like
evenings in the cover of algae
on the far shore
Surmai Shaamein!

-: Evening-Morning :-

The evening is
surrounded by bright
pink color, sunny sparkling.
Moving away from
some distance on
the black stone,
your existence was
waving taking
the whole creation
in its arms.
O Majestic!
You are together
the blue sky roof,
in the house of
marbled walls -
The evening has
entered, shining
behind the pink curtain
of the evening,
your bright beam
like the sun.
An innocent smile

has been drawn
like a line
on your lips.
The paintbrush
of silence
on the canvas
of your lips –
Spreading eternal
color…. As if the
crimson lines
of the sun are
weaving a weft,
and the red fiery
flowers are falling.
In the ocean
of this dusk,
the sky-evening
has bathed,
wiped the body with
the crimson rays,
weaving the wefts
of the rays, has
made another
evening—morning.

-: Gray evenings !!! :-

Years have passed
since you left,
the reach of your arms
has gone away.
A sad poem
came to
on the lips
and it's floating
upon the water
flowing on the Sky.
Gray evenings
reflected on
the river
Boats of the boatmen
Are crossing the horizon.
Come again
Dear!
The sails
are set,

the moon

is blooming,

Is Beyond the horizon -

our meeting

Beyond the horizon -

is our Peace!

Love Affair (Dil Dariya Hai)

Part (2)

-Last installment

String of lights in the garden of mind; Holi decorated on the colorful wings of union; drops frozen in the foggy nights, and aliphatic showers on the lazy youth in summer, were decorating the pages of hopes and expectations. The entire poetry of life could not be his, but the meaning of some words of the meeting could be found. Sophia's husband could turn Samina's life's summer into spring. The burning feeling of absence could have become mountain's air, but the husband of Sophia's sister, alias Sameena's husband, did not have that fire in his chest, there was not enough coal that could incinerate the absence by becoming a flame. No equation could overwhelm with richness.

The district library which was near the house became indifferent followed by the irresponsibility of the husband and the crippling hunger of the children. Alas! Images kept on getting created and spoiled on the memory board. With 'anything could happen; don't get discouraged, Nishant was standing with a simple smile. His lips were trembling. He was the hero of Hindi novels seen through the windows of the pages.

Rupali Bhatt
30/08/2008

Dark clouds had gathered around and both of them were walking slowly. The rain had not stopped yet, the destination was far away; there were drizzling drops, and the rain was falling drop by drop from the hair of Sameena. Nishant's trembling hand slid over Sameena's shoulder. Two shadows got lost in the darkness without being aware. What kind of relationship this is; unknown and the closest. Sameena could neither rest her head on the shoulders of sister Sophia's fraudster husband nor on the chest of her husband Shahid. Life was sliding on the sand, when Nishant handed her the appointment letter.

Working in the library, Sameena's life became normal. Now those bends and cuts were no longer there which used to bleed Sameena's body and mind. The ordeals of life were over. Now a garden had blossomed in the courtyard of the mind.

While narrating the story of her life, Sameena kept on asking about the life she passed... Age after age, the evenings kept getting drenched in the shower of questions and she kept on saying who is really to be blamed for the lives lived in this way — the society, the woman or man?

-: ......And I hummed your name! :-

Waited for you
on a sulky evening
the letter that was written,
The answer from the ambience
came for you.
Perhaps your home
is right here
on the high hill,
the darkness
has come
slipping like sand.
Thick as ink
has settled
around my house.
One can't
see the way
far and wide.

I used to
get scared of
the shadows
of midnight,
I used to break down
and scatter,
but on this hillock,
a speck of
light shines,
Maybe this is
your stormy face.
Your face shines in
the dark circle
of the night like
a bright gem,
Your stormy face
came to me
like a ray of light.
I found it
in the slow
morning.
The letters

which used

to be pictorial –

I have composed

these songs

with ink on paper.

I have

hummed more,

your name again

with my lips.

And the centuries' darkness of my mind was

extinguished.

-: Ghost of Love :-

He
followed
me under
the row
of trees.
Ducks
swimming
in the lake,
The water
was green
like the ocean;
Moss on
the sediment,
gray fish
and vines
around
banyan tree.
Tall

date palms
and thorny
trees
rare,
Eucalyptus
and
Ashoka
simple.
Mango
Tamarind clumps
Pigeons,
rabbits
and chameleons.
He used to
wait
for me
under
the bush
of blue
yellow
flowers
and

bamboo
tree,
Full of
love
taking
his hand
in mine.
So many
matter
used
to happen,
untold,
Speechless! Speechless!

-: ......And an era passed :-

I drank every moment,
Lived every moment,
Your dripping spirituality,
And your intoxicating eyes.
From new life to life,
And the cups of the lips,
I drank every moment,
Lived every moment,

To the thorny appearance
And the flavor of the overflowing body
I drank every moment,
Lived every moment.
From the intoxicating pitcher of youth,
And the intoxicating liquor,
I drank every moment,
Lived every moment.

......And an era passed.

-: As the evening starts :-

This sinking image fruit,
this fruit of the sky,
behind the rows of eucalyptus,
is decorated on the
the forehead of the evening.
The paths walk side by side,
parting at the bend,
where a bunch of Burrus
has grown.
Sitting here on
the gray rock,
I had seen the sun-set
together,
on the sights of carpet
greenery had grown.
Branches and branches
Had turned into the embrace
of your body.

While gathering
my thoughts,
a dark night had
appeared on the
canvas of the sky.
Poli soil
sinking feet,
saying something
while stopping.
While listening,
on the pinnacle,
the moonlight
had risen.
The solid youth
of the trees,
the flowing river,
the swaying vines,
the curly tresses of
the banyans hanging
on the dusty wall.
The loop of our arms kept

loosening, and the
paths kept
getting separated….
Lost in a densely
populated city that
had become intense,
and static
was lost in the screams
of the chirping,
in the uncivilized sound,
Disappeared into the
Hustle bustle of the city.

-: Innocent life :-

Don’t know why
I kept passing
by your side,
I didn’t regain my senses,
I kept getting down.
There was a caravan
at the turn itself –
I left it
I am coming back
on your path.
The flower of the face
has blossomed
so much youth
is getting
flared up
on the lips of fire
The attraction of love
is getting destroyed

in the fire
The innocent life
is getting better
again and again.
Today, I have sent my
message to you,
It is the season
of merriment.
I have sent the
consequence.
Raining stars are
in my head,
I have sent
a message
to your lips.
Don't be late,
come soon,
your and mine
way should
remain close;
Don't get
Separated.

-: Shanti :-

The silence was now beginning to spread; dusk had fallen deeply. Flocks of wings of white clouds were scattered on the horizon. The sinking crimson fruit of the sky was spreading a pink tint on the wings of clouds. The evening was bathed in wonderful colors by nature's brush. Now the scene behind the hill had become golden, and the web of moving rays was spreading the aura of yellow-brown colors. The water of the hill flowing down at a slow speed was in golden colour like sandalwood. Shanti was sitting in a hut behind a clump of bushes. In the dim light of the lamp burning on the cauldron kept upside down in front of her, her black lips were matching with the now spreading darkness. She put off the fire but heat was still there.

The first meeting of her confluence journey with Bablu took place at Banke's modernly decorated clothes showroom when their eyes met and the eyelids drooped, and then the process of meeting began, along Gwalior Road, Elite and flickered from toy talkies to gardens. Bablu's budding youth, madness, repeating the lines of film songs with enthusiasm, taking Shanti in his arms, swearing of life and death went on freely and unabatedly. Falling in love with that man became a boon to the colorless life of that woman, whose husband used to catch a bird every day with whom he would spend days of physical relationship and then drive the bird away. Birds were of so many colors; white, black, golden-winged, blue-yellow wings, sometimes wrapped in the pallu of a saree and sometimes fluttering in the modern environment. He used to love someone, buy someone, bring someone in into marriage, and used to make the world aware of the colourful life of a man. Shanti's husband had no shortage of money. From Banarasi sarees to air travel was a part of her life, but this air of external respect was suffocating Shanti every moment. Shanti's flames of restlessness got coolness from the fountains of love showered from the bottom of the heart by Bablu, which irrigated the blue-yellow flowers of the garden of her mind and body.

Gently lifting the chin of Shanti's tear-filled face, Bablu said, 'Let us run away somewhere, then we will establish a new world.'

'Get off! What will the world and society say?'

What do you have to do with the world and society; it is neither of happiness nor sorrow. My dear, I will give you every pleasure; I will do anything for you. The rhythm of the movie song, *Chal Chameli Bagh Mein...* started floating on Bablu's lips. Shanti laughed spontaneously and Bablu started kissing her youthful body with his lips. Shanti's dusky body started to sigh and exhale. The bumps started vibrating and the moon started dissolving its light in the canal flowing behind

that gray wall and the whole canal became milky. … Now was neither moon nor night. The earthy wall had turned brown. in the light of day. Shanti fixed her clothes and Bablu kissed her on the forehead and vowed not to be anyone else's for the rest of her life. For some time both of them kept looking at each other, then the woman hugged the man to her chest. She was placed at that stage of life where she had to stay and rest.

Today, Shanti was alone at home. Clad in a raw silk saree, holding her chin with her hand, she was sitting on the floor, combing her hair. The husband was missing for two days, probably traveling with some colorful bird. Shanti got up and moved the curtain and started looking out of the window. Evening had come, cumulus clouds were hovering, and a flock of birds chirped together and flew floating in the sky above. She filled the open air inside in one breath, then exhaled and left it. Aah! It's been fourteen years, bearing the suffocation inherited from this pompous society, carrying these strong feelings and wearing the cloak of husband's name, and carrying those rituals whose weight of the past had shaken the present. She remembered the brass plate decorated with dry fruits on the fruit platter, which her brother had brought and what not her parents had given her, she had spent freely. With what pomp and show she was married. She was standing dressed as a bride and auspicious songs were being sung. Circumstances didn't leave time for all these things, didn't justify them. It would have been difficult for her to breathe in the suffocating cloud of this atmosphere if she had not got the support of Bablu. Bablu had become her support. She wanted to repeat this take again and again and wanted to complete the music of the song of life. Dusk had almost set in. When she looked away, the moon, dressed in light clouds, was sitting on the scaffolding of the sky, protected from Earth's stormy dust and natural upheavals. Shanti too was safe in the lap of a man, from the savaged animals of this earth and the sorrows of the soulless world. The moon was standing in its place showering affectionate rays. There was so much similarity, for example, between the two of them. There was a sound of someone at the door. Shanti was startled and said, 'Who is it?'

'Bablu! Open it!!"

Shanti retorted, 'At this time?'

'There is no point in this also when the lovers get a chance to meet,' Bablu said gleefully.

"Yes, all is well, but... you come in," said Shanti, and when Bablu came in, she bolted the door.

'Sit down and have tea that I am preparing with cardamom. You like it very much.'

Bablu caught hold of Shanti's hand and peeping into her prickly eyes with his left side, said, 'Uh, sit here, I will drink liquor from your hands, I will drink so much that I will not be conscious and will become intoxicated after heavy drinking.'

Almost releasing her hand, Shanti said, 'If you want to drink, drink from my eyes only, I am not going to come close to you.'

Bablu went ahead and embraced her completely and started looking at her with very loving eyes. Giving a soft kiss on her lips, he said, 'I feel like sacrificing my whole life for you. Be with you forever, sweetheart! So this drinking habit should be dropped forever.' Shanti picked up a bottle of beer from her husband's bar and put the bottle on the table and said with a grimace, 'Bablu later, you will have to stop drinking this liquor while living with me.'

'I will stop drinking, Baba, I will stop. I will leave everything but I will not leave you.'

'Now you have the enthusiasm of youth, then I am much older than you, the age of the tenderness of the organs will also pass soon, will you die for me like this? Will you change or time will change you,' said the woman standing under the canopy of that night, thinking of the land of daylight. She said this after looking at the lonely sky, where even a search could not find a piece of soaking cloud.

Bablu wrapped her in his arms and said, 'You have become mad at this age. You are prettier than a 16-year-old, don't say such things ever again.' That night she surrendered herself to those arms; Shanti was drenched. With sips of wine, both immersed themselves in ecstasy. The ecstasy of the man and the woman was disturbed when there was a midnight knock on the door and the husband of the Shanti entered the house. The heroes and heroines courting within the walls of the house were not of such a high standard, nor were they so educated, that Bablu jumped off the sloping roof and ran away. Shanti's husband heard the sound of someone jumping from the floor. A beer bottle was lying rolled over on the table. A man's shirt was tied on a nearby peg which was not his. Then he started talking harshly, 'bastard bitch, with whom you were fornicating? Didn't you feel ashamed of drowning my and this house's respect? For many days I have been hearing about your debauchery from neighbours and others. Witch, now stop these escapades,' saying this, Shanti's husband kicked her.

'What respect and religion are you talking about, you had already auctioned your faith with the prostitutes. Now you are posing a conscientious man,' said Shanti in one breath and today the suffocation of her life turned into terror and aggression and now she wanted to end them too. She punched Suvedar's nose. Subedar writhed in agony. 'Bastard, you are betraying the one who feeds you. Bastard, how dare you, even after doing something wrong you don't show an ounce of shame or regret,' saying this, he ran to the door towards Shanti. Shanti had put the chain on it from outside and he kept on fussing, unsuccessfully. Shanti had gone away, leaving the house forever or the decorated house had forgotten it forever and the householder was just an excuse. The house had now become a ruin for her, Shanti, tired of years, left her husband's wealth, gold, silver and jewelry in its walls so that no sorrows should come along. She did not consider it appropriate to bring anything along.

After walking some distance, she sat under the shade of a banyan tree. She was tired and the folds of her sari also wanted to relax. Her body was breaking and the darkness of the night was falling on her body. In that fearful silence, she took under the shelter of a giant banyan tree. She too had become a calm banyan. Slowly the darkness of the night was receding and the journey of the sun was starting with pink color. She was still in her sleep when the light of the day shone on her body; she got up in a hurry. The rays of the sun were coming down from her face and were shimmering in her chest. The sweat points were shining on the chest, which were being fed by the strings of the sun's rays like threads, making like a necklace of pearls.

The hustle and bustle of the day had begun. Meanwhile Bablu had come to the corner of the G.I.C. road. He used to go to Banke's clothes' showroom. At a distance of about one and a half furlongs, away from the side of the road, Shanti was sitting under a garden of mango trees. Bablu's mind was overwhelmed on seeing her. After getting down from the road, he stood leaning on the front rock. Here, Shanti saw the shadow of a man and after recognizing him, she hugged him and said, 'Bablu, I have left everything behind, yes everything, the house of that useless and unmanly man. My world has been plundered; now, you are everything to me.' Saying this, she cried hugging Bablu. Bablu stood in her embrace for some time, and after consoling her, could say barely, 'But where will I keep you; I myself spend the night in the stable. How will you be able to live there?'

'We will take a one-room house somewhere which will be a temple of our love; you and I will be the deities of that temple. Even when we are not there, there will be two tomb stones and people will come from far and wide to pray. We will eat *dal-roti* and build a world of love,' Shanti said eagerly.

'But I don't have money at the moment,' he said, assuring Shanti. 'It will come, then we will build the cottage by adding brick-by-brick. Thatched roof will be there and the fence of the clump of bush will cover both of us,' Bablu said almost squeezing her in the chest. There were ebb and flow in Shanti's fleshy body…

Both went to their old acquaintance Mrs. Shastri's place, either to celebrate their freedom or to seek shelter. Shastri ji was working as an Assistant Lecturer in a technical department. His wife was a devoted homemaker. Had two children, a son and a daughter. Both were young. Seeing Bablu and Shanti together and listening to their story, they both were highly surprised. Bablu went out to smoke *beedi* and Shanti sat beside the well-built housewife.

‘Hey Shanti, you have destroyed your house,’ she said.

‘What could I have done with that person? Not even for a day, he did not look at me with love. He was just busy amorously with other women.’

‘You could have tried to tackle the issue with some discussion and understanding with him but you have drowned yourself in the intoxication. You will repent for this in future.’

Shanti said smiling and winking, ‘It is better to get intoxicated in this toxicity than burning in that embers.’

‘What do you know about bonding? You landed from one painful situation to another. Now that you have come, call Bablu inside and have food.’ Then she called out to her daughter Radha, ‘Daughter Radha, bring some hot tea.’ ....Shanti did not understand much of Mrs. Shastri’s words, she was just engrossed in starting a new life. She said to Mrs. Shastri, ‘If you could get a room here, it would be a great favour. I know you for a long time.’

‘Now, there is no room, the house is full; some land is lying vacant outside, you put something on it,’ Mrs. Shastri said.

From the second day onwards, Bablu and Shanti’s thatched-roofed brick-on-brick chin huts started being built under the cover of clumps of bushes. May be, it was the palace of her dreams. From then till today, behind the cover of those bushes, her dreams of palace not created, rather get shattered. She kept on earning a small quantity of food that is not sufficient and kept looking at her past, present and future in dark evenings. She kept watching her life like a serialized episodes of a movie. Time kept passing by, all of Bablu's promises were finished under his habit of drinks, and their survival was managed with Shanti's earnings.

It is said-

The funeral pyre

of union is raised

on the bed of religion.

***

Whom does it suit to

love like Radhakrishna?

People just like

to worship them.

But keeping aside the ostentatiousness and conceit created by the people, the women like Shanti even dared to make her own and choose lovers even as the men who loved them continued to betray. She had left all the money with her ex-husband earlier. It didn't deem her fit to bring even a penny from someone who did not respect the sanctity of marriage, but from some perspective, it seemed to her that it was absolutely inappropriate; she should have taken money that belonged to her, and as she was later told by educated people that she had a right to do so. She got carried away in feminine feelings, probably because of being illiterate. Everyone said lot many things to her, but she didn't know what was right and what was wrong? As an illiterate, unaware of the worldly knowledge, she was unable to find out the requisite basic things and understand the significance of materials to carry on with life. Someone explained to her that even as Bablu had been living with you, you never formally married him. You can claim your alimony case on that unruly husband, but neither Shanti had the money for the court proceedings, nor could her life-weary brain think of any way; the court proceedings were a distant dream for her.

Bablu used to come late, drunken and after quenching his sexual thirst from Shanti, he used to lay down. Even the young body of the woman eagerly supported him. After some times, Bablu would regain his senses and would utter abusively, 'Give me food...'. 'It is ready.' Shanti would say, moving the plate forward, 'Take it.' Then giving a glass of water, she asked, 'Did you get some money from the shop today?'

'No!'

'Why?'

‘As you are already earning, so I have stopped working there. Give me some money for tomorrow’s drink. Tomorrow there will be a card game with my friends, I will definitely win in that, then I will bring you not one but two silk sarees. Yes, give me, my dear.’ Bablu was staggering because he had drunk a lot. Then he said in an indistinct voice, ‘I don’t go anywhere and I will not go anywhere, my dear’ and he started running his hand over Shanti’s body and started showering kisses. Fire started on both sides and as a typical woman, Shanti surrendered to him. She lay down for a while, then got up and put fifty rupees on Bablu’s hand. Bablu kissed her little dark but soft lips and fell asleep peacefully.

Till now Shanti used to work as a labourer. Now she has taken up the work of cleaning utensils and mopping job in few houses. When she got tired of working as a labourer, then she would sell vegetables in a basket on her head. One day, when Shanti returned in the evening, there was pain in her body, and had fever too. She lay down in the hut. She used to cook food every day after returning from work; she would prepare food even while going to work. She couldn’t get up today because of fever. Bablu returned after playing cards and asked for food. Shanti said, ‘Today I can’t do. So you make *roti*, and vegetable is cooked and ready.’

‘So, now I will become a woman and prepare *roti*. Get up and cook food for me and give money too, I don't have a penny left.' Today, after hearing this, Shanti got irritated and thought for how long she would continue to bear the brunt of being a woman. She said in a loud and full voice, 'If you are a real man, then show it by taking care of me, not by snatching money.I am not your slave that I should always obey for what you say.' Bablu pushed her back to the wall and tried to kiss her on her lips, but today Shanti pushed him away. The leaves of the peepal tree standing outside rattled and started telling the story of the darkness that came down into the world. Religion and bondage encourages a woman to perform her duty only, to perform it efficiently, to perform her duty completely even if she does not get love in return. In this world of men, where does the love of man and woman succeed? Even in this scenario, the flag of man's pressure remains high, when a woman falls in love, she leaves with no option but to wail.

Today, Shanti got infuriated. She said, 'Today I will not give you even a penny.' Bablu grabbed the stick lying nearby and started beating Shanti. Hearing the screams, Mrs. Shastri came out of the house and while scolding Bablu, she intervened, and stopped fight between them. 'Hey Ram, how these people are!' she muttered to herself.

The silence of the night spread. Bablu rolled and slept over on one side; crickets' chirping sound could be heard for some distance. Banana trees in front looked like a statue. Shanti also resembled it. Neither was there any presence of air, nor was there movement in the body of Shanti, but there was a mind that could not stop; it was wandering far and wide, the sound of the whistle of the train passing through the nearby crossing was also heard in the distance. The sheet of darkness stretched all around, but her mind was searching for a corner of light. Perhaps that corner could have been obtained by seeking shelter from her first husband. Till midnight, waves and echoes of chorus music of *Bundelkhandi folk* dance continued to come from the rural areas.

Early in the morning, Shanti got up and washed her face. She tried to finish the daily household chores. Bablu was sleeping pronely. She walked towards the nearby medical store. Then she went ahead and bought a silk saree from the hawker and rushed towards her first husband's house. Her husband, Subedar, pushed her to clean his entire house and pasted cow dung on the courtyard, and then he handed over some money to her, but he refused to keep Shanti with him.

With a long face, Shanti came back to her hut. The raw walls of the hut laughed and fell asleep, silence stretched but sleep was far away from the eyes of Shanti. Radha, the elder daughter of Mrs. Shastri, who was working on her thesis till late night, started thinking about the situation of Shanti. Pressing the pages with a paper weight, she leaned on the chair. Mrs. Shastri brought a glass of milk for her daughter who was

studying. Radha opened the screen of the window. The canopy of the new moon was fixed on the bed sheet of the night. Radha emptied the glass of milk and looking at her mother, said, 'Perhaps if Shanti had been educated, she could have found a better option for life. How poor she is despite being today's woman. Generally, all these compulsions pass on the women of the labouring class. Still, if we look at today's educated women, they get firm economic and other supports, but if we look after removing the curtains, there is no guarantee of how much protection is there from the life partner.'

Mrs. Shastri shook her head dejectedly thinking of the bitter truths she had swallowed.

The second daughter, Namita, who was half-lying on the bed with a pillow, was a final year student of law at Bundelkhand University, Jhansi, said in a slightly intense voice, 'As long as a woman needs the crutch of a man, even if she resorts to change all the men, she will never be able to stand on her own. Till the day she will recognize herself and stand on her own which will be only hers. Let she breathe in atmospheric freedom (open air) and laugh heartily.

Here, she is born not only to live but also to be happy, but nobody knows how much the people who keep women in bondage will agree.' The blackness of the night was spreading around the hut and the buildings. Now more and more silence had spread. In the midst of this floating silence, the chorus of *Bundelkhandi folk* songs could be heard coming closer.

Shanti awoke before dawn. She had to go to for shoveling, return and to prepare the kitchen and fulfill Bablu ji's desires; otherwise, the proud and arrogant Bablu would kill her mercilessly.

After getting up, she got busy with all the work and Bablu was singing drunkenly.

'Python doesn't serve,

Birds don't work.

Lord Rama is the bestower of all,

Said Das Maluka.'

Section
'B'

-: Destinations are not easy :-

There is sky, there is flight
and flapping wings to fly.
Feet get stuck in the mud,
sometimes on the hot floor,
Sometimes walk alone.

-: Holi :-

Let the clean bodice becomes
full of stains.
Let someone plays Holi
like this with me, but
then every ugly stain
is not a colour.

-: Destinations :-

Destinations are not achieved like this
Destiney also plays its part,
God's treasure-trove is here;
It is a story of lines.
From where should I get hope?
Life is sulking,
His list of dreams
Is faltering.

-: Heart's Desire :-

Dew drops on the face
No skylark there.
Emotions arise
from the lips.
Dusty environment is
All around
But it looks,
There is no caravan.
Shining hairs are on the
Surface of the sand,
But no deer
Is thirsty.
Your name came
On the lips, but
The past moments
Betrayed me.
To what extent
The gamblers played,

But they couldn't
Get anyone.
Let our desire of mind
Bloom,
And get us completely
Drenched.
But no one could find
Such an Indra.